BLACK AND WHITE

for Eleanor, Lydia, Blanche, Barbara And Robert 1985

First published in Great Britain by
Pelham Books Ltd
27 Wrights Lane
Kensington
London W8 5DZ
1986

British Library Cataloguing in Publication Data
Hughes, David
Black and white.
I. Title
823'.914 [F]   PR6058.U3/

ISBN 0–7207–1699–3

PRINTED IN BELGIUM BY
proost
INTERNATIONAL BOOK PRODUCTION

BLACK AND WHITE

Written and illustrated by David Hughes

PELHAM BOOKS

I'm Bird

I'm Cat

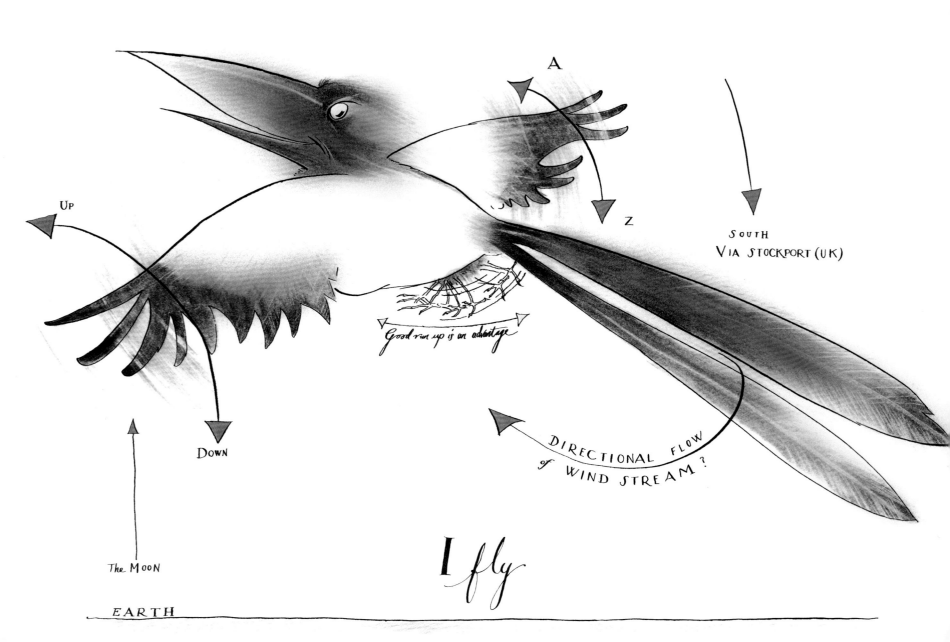

A

Z

Up

Down

The MOON

EARTH

SOUTH
VIA STOCKPORT (UK)

Good run up is an advantage

DIRECTIONAL FLOW
of WIND STREAM?

I fly

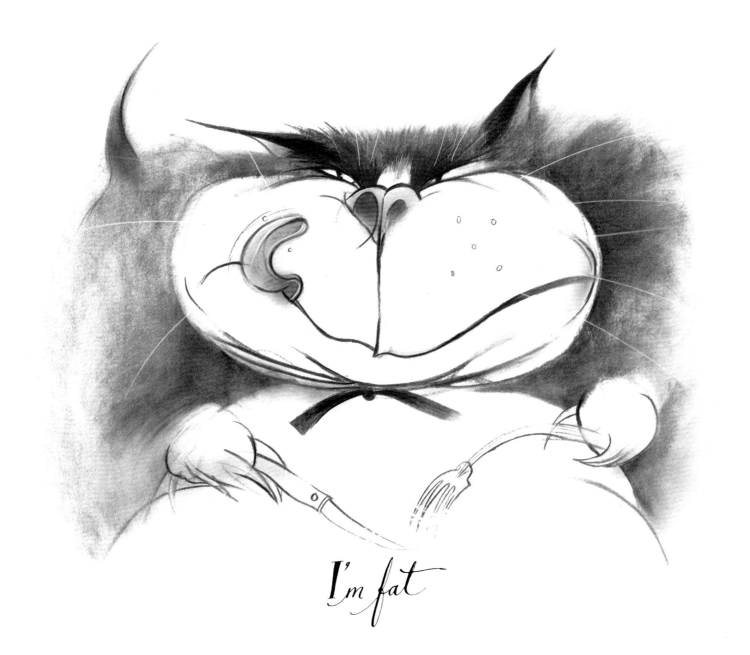

I'm fat

I like worms

I've got wings

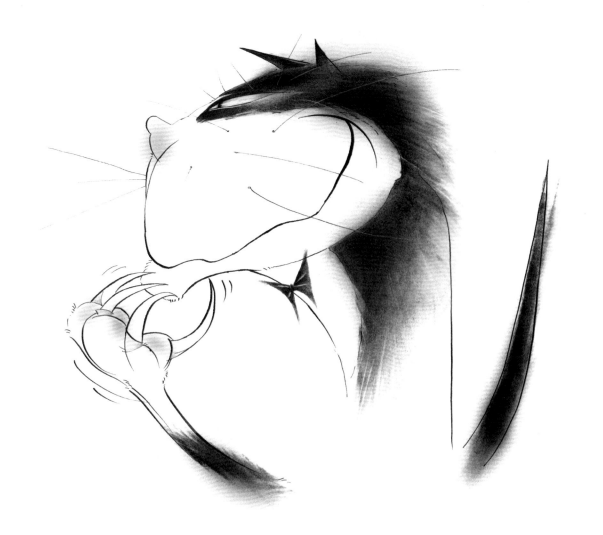

I've got claws

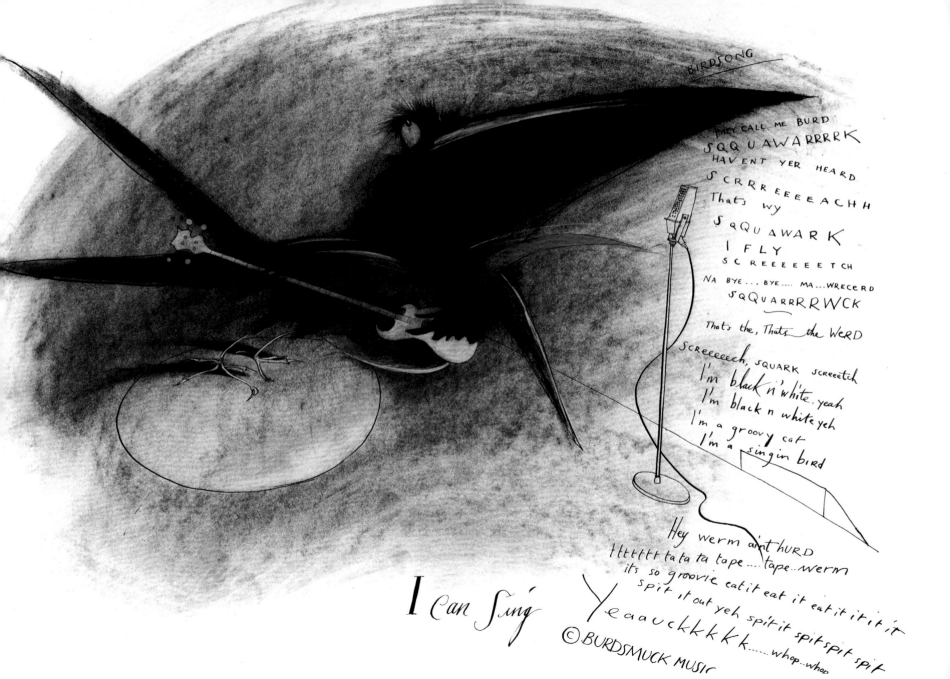

BIRDSONG

THEY CALL ME BURD
SQQUAWARRRRK
HAVENT YER HEARD
SCRRREEEEACHH
Thats wy
SQQUAWARK
I FLY
SCREEEEEETCH
NA BYE... BYE.... MA...WRECERD
SQQUARRRRWCK

Thats the, Thats the WERD

screeeeech, SQUARK screeetch
I'm black n'white, yeah
I'm black n white yeh
I'm a groovy cat
I'm a singin bird

Hey werm aint HURD
ttttttt ta ta ta tape....tape...werm
its so groovie eat it eat it eat it it it it
spit it out yeh spit it spit spit spit

I Can Sing   Yeaauckkkkk.....whop..whop

©BURDSMUCK MUSIC

FROM A GREAT HEIGHT.
(A)

(B)

Earth

I land on all fours

I'm Bird!

I'm Cat

I've got a mate

I stay out late

I lay eggs

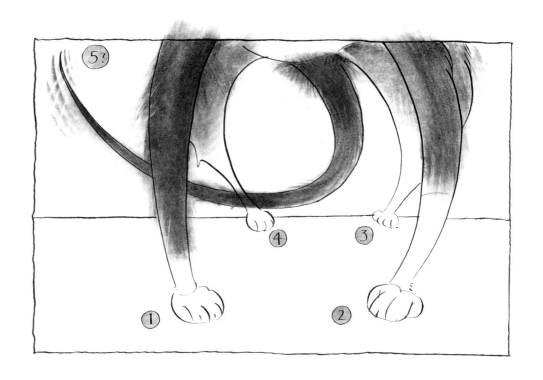

I've got four legs

I live in a nest

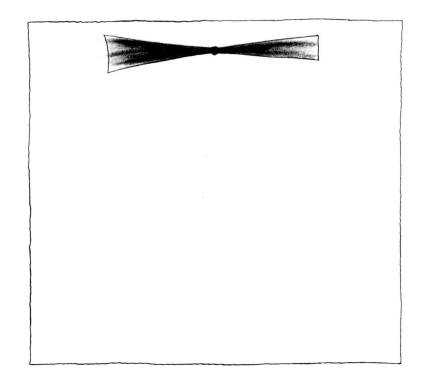

I've got a white chest

I hide in trees

I've got 3000 fleas

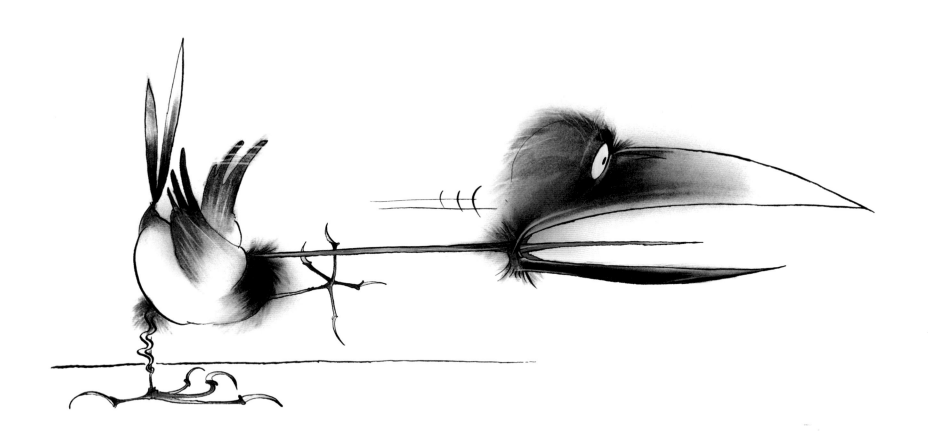

I'm BIRDD!

I'm cat

I've got feathers

I've got fur

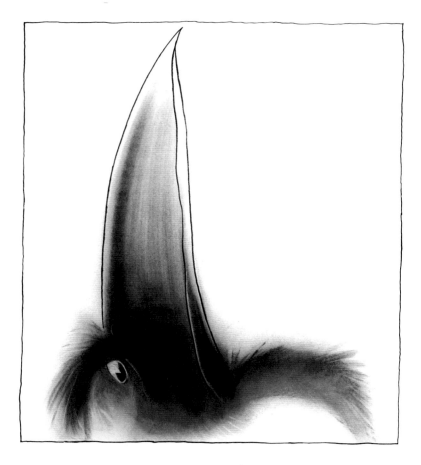

I've a beak

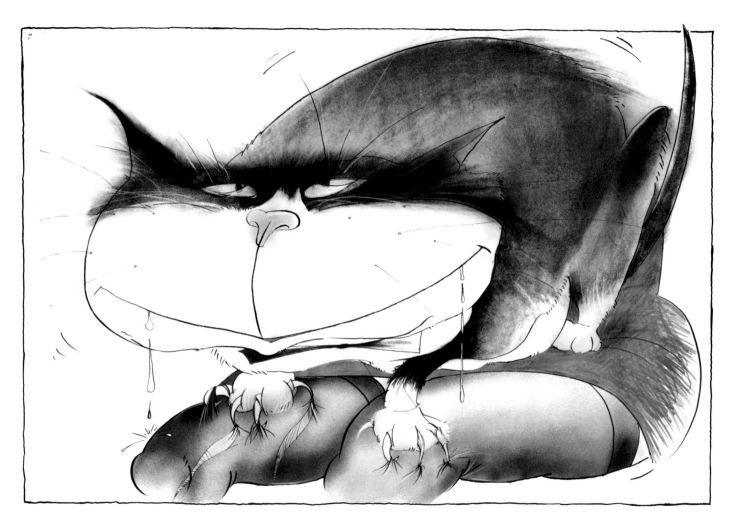

I can purr

I like a natter

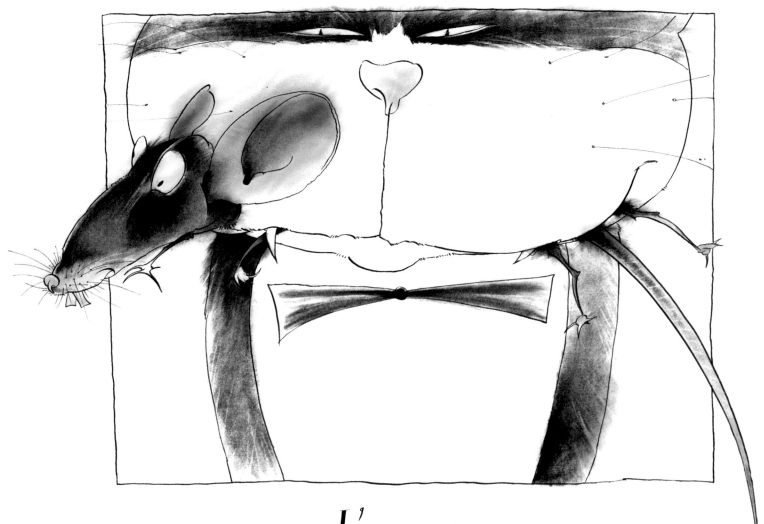

I'm a ratter

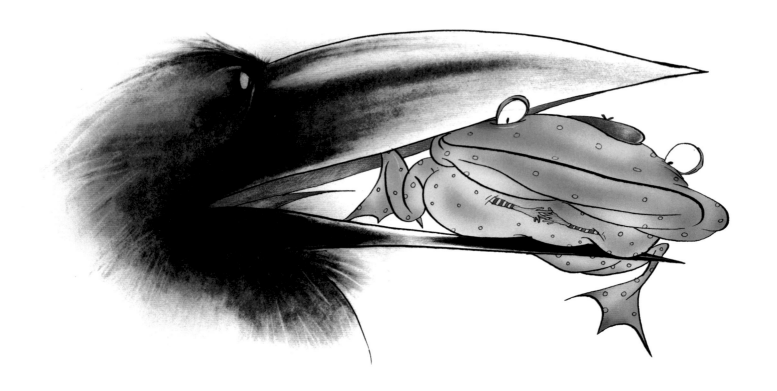

I eat frogs

I scratch dogs

I'm BBURRD!

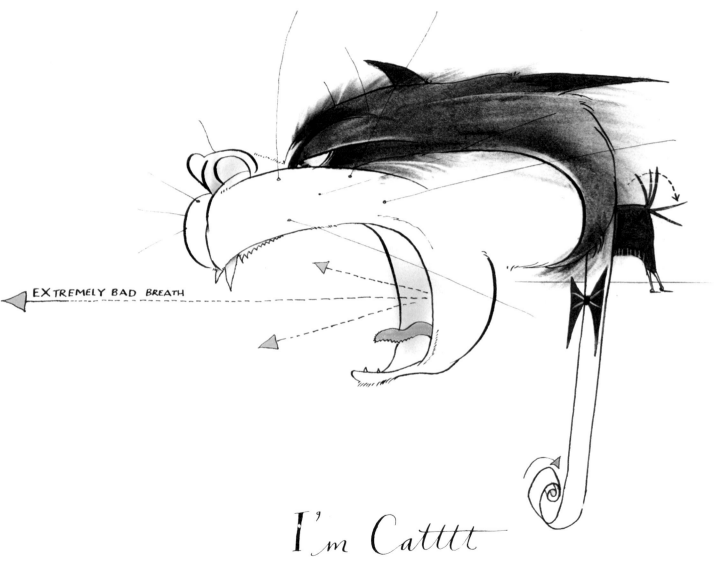

EXTREMELY BAD BREATH

I'm Catttt

I've got beady eyes

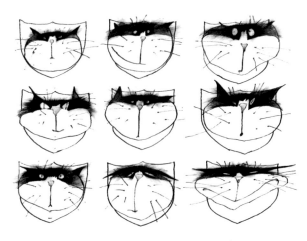

I've got nine lives

I ferry it

I bury it

I'm black and white

I'm white and black

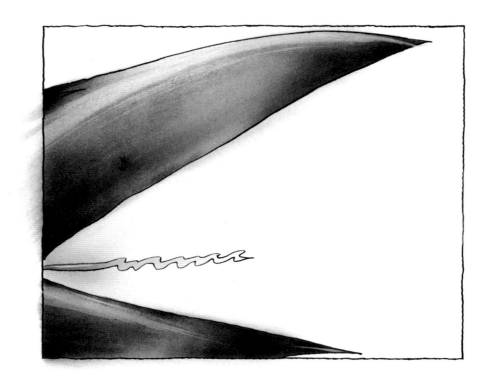

I'm BBBBUURRRRD!

You're absurd!

I'm fat

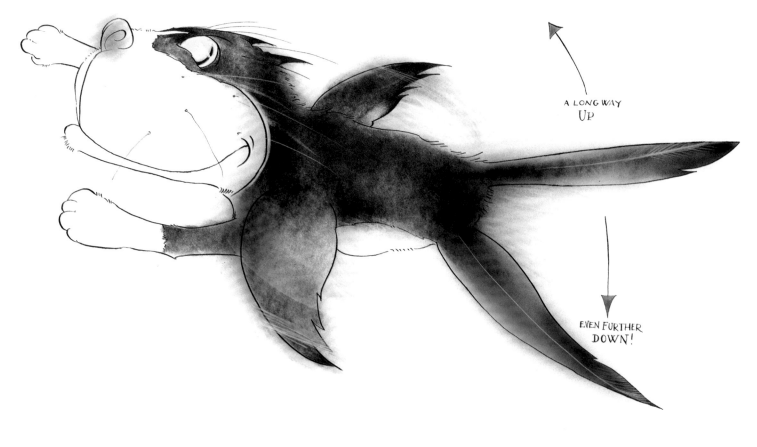

A LONG WAY
UP

EVEN FURTHER
DOWN!

CONCRETE

I fly

I've got four legs

I lay eggs

I've got fur

I've got feathers

I'm Bird

I'm cat

I can purr

I've a beak

I live in a nest

I've got nine lives

I'm Wonderful

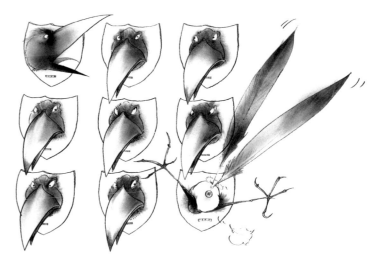

I'm best

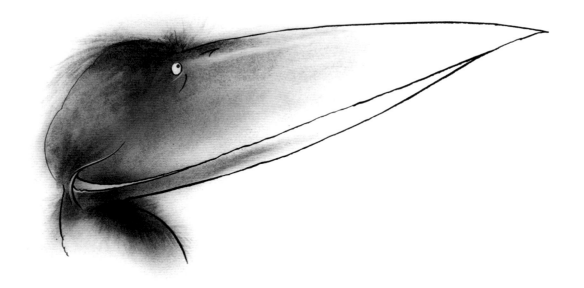

I'm Bird

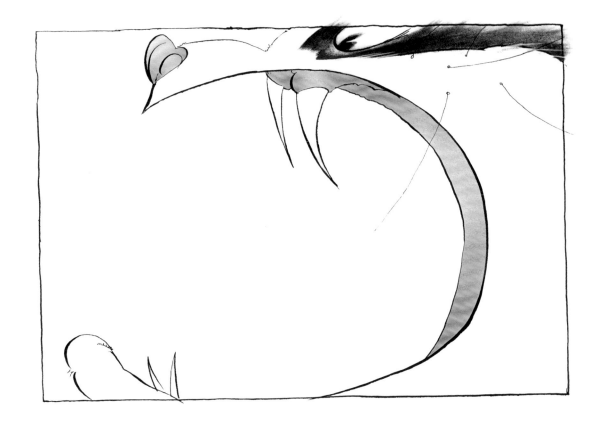

I'm KKCCATTTT!

I'm black and white

I'm black and white

I've got a tail

Mine's the longest

I can fly

I ate a Magpie

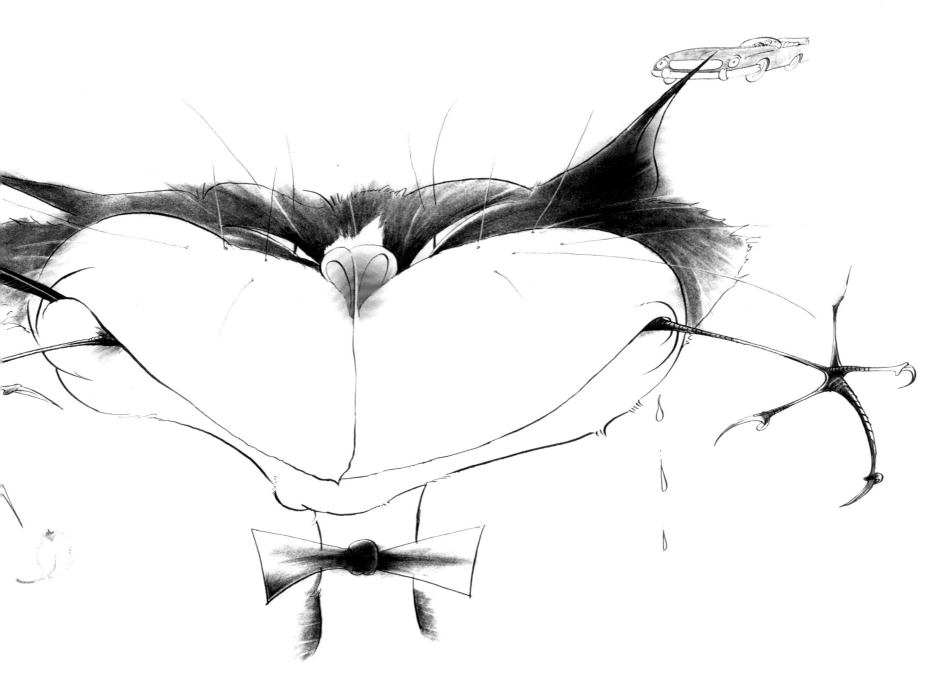

I'm Fin

I'm Flat

I'll have some of THAT !